TURNCOAT

Cover art by John O'Brian
Cover design by Laura Joakimson

Cover typeface: Abril Fatface and Academy Engraved LET
Interior typeface: Garamond Premier Pro
Interior design by Laura Joakimson & Sophia Carr

Library of Congress Cataloging-in-Publication Data

Names: Bendall, Molly, author.
Title: Turncoat / Molly Bendall.
Description: Oakland, California : Omnidawn Publishing, 2025. |
Summary:
"Through the poems in Turncoat, Molly Bendall's sixth collection, the speaker and other figures dwell under the ever-present eye of surveillance by unspecified authorities. Mistrust and dread become part of the fabric of their lives, as they never know who may be a turncoat-a person who disguises her allegiances and traffics in betrayal. These poems employ an invented paranoid syntax meant to evade oppressive surveillance. A series of intimate and darkly humorous incidents press the speaker to continually adapt to unseen-or even nonexistent-dangers. Haunted by a sense of disorientation and uncertainty about whether old friendships may have been compromised, or if spaces could disappear overnight, Bendall's poems coax the reader to step across boundaries and snares, alternating between episodes of interrogation and flight"--
Provided by publisher.
Identifiers: LCCN 2025016175 | ISBN 9781632431691 (trade paperback ; acid-free paper)
Subjects: LCGFT: Poetry.
Classification: LCC PS3552.E5384 T87 2025 | DDC 811/.54--dc23/eng/20250411
LC record available at https://lccn.loc.gov/2025016175

Published by Omnidawn Publishing, Oakland, California
www.omnidawn.com
10 9 8 7 6 5 4 3 2 1
ISBN: 978-1-63243-169-1

In the exquisite, enigmatic, finely calibrated poems of *Turncoat*, Molly Bendall plumbs the deep sense of unease running just under the surface of twenty-first-century life. "I barely saw," her speaker reports, "the future behind us." Terse yet expansive, disjointed yet seamless, these poems fashion a mode, and a world, entirely Bendall's. Don't ask how she wrote these stunning poems—just read them, and have your mind quietly blown.
—Donna Stonecipher, author of *The Ruins of Nostalgia*

The poems in Molly Bendall's *Turncoat* inhabit a world where the difference between being watched and being the watcher no longer exists. Paranoia abounds as Bendall creates a syntax all her own: "how do I register myself. / am I beating. / is air leaving my mouth?"
—Eloisa Amezcua, author of *Fighting Is Like a Wife*

Molly Bendall's fascinating and challenging new collection, *Turncoat*, leads us into "The Vague Territory of the Present." Bendall makes us unnervingly aware of how enmeshed in a surveillance society we already are: "Calculating now what's permissible, and what / we're barred from even considering." But within the straitjacket of repression, Bendall enacts a Houdini-like escape. Her restless erudition and formal skill shape and reshape identity: "I'd invent a stitch for my sentence so its pulse would skip." It's in those syncopated gaps that the turncoat resurges as an agent of resistance.
—Elizabeth Robinson, author of *Excursive*

Previous Books

WATCHFUL
Omnidawn Publishing, 2016

BLING & FRINGE (Co-authored with Gail Wronsky)
What Books, 2009

UNDER THE QUICK
Parlor Press, 2009

ARIADNE'S ISLAND
Miami University Press, 2002

DARK SUMMER
Miami University Press, 1999

AFTER ESTRANGEMENT
Peregrine Smith Books, 1992

TURNCOAT

Molly Bendall

Omnidawn Publishing
Oakland, California
2025

CONTENTS

I

II

I

And now blindness was being peddled on this red evening in the city, with glass eyes for everyone.

Herta Müller

Confidential Meeting for Future Reference

I can't decide
if the monument I stand beside
arrests me, or if it
pushes me too close
to blood traveling my arteries,
slow, but language sparks
when I quicken it
the rollcall
and the birds argue non-stop
I'd serve and serve them—
here are my eyes
my unbuttoned forehead
now the stairwell
carries no daylight
and the mayor wanders
the back streets—do we
forbid ourselves
from carrying purses
with tissues and powder?

the building shook
from the bottom and later
when I heard them
through the transom,
I knew and followed
in my apprentice suit
I make shields
and fold maps
into chicken craws
I stuff a grab bag
of delight
I'm expected
with meals for them
thunder stumbles up the steps—
no more bargaining
it's when my sweater fills
with air then with water
that morning comes
to the quiet streets of power.

Don't turn around, I'm not here

For all the help in the city. My face switched off.
I'd spin the attention to the backs of my knees. Between
thoughts, even between swallows. Drop all ranks.
Questioning is a ten-day business. Whether I differed from
one night. Luxury buildings stood half-open. Since the working
day couldn't. The scaffolding and a show of a door stitched on.
Thumbtacked for the following spring. You start with the locals.
Turn yourselves into birds. He pressed—too far-fetched for an opening.
Can't tell speaking from thinking. From the get-go the buildings
would retire. Postponed again. Keys chime on the concrete.
Could be as long as sympathy's untended. If thoughts strayed,
swap a buckle for some flesh. My knees shy of objects.
A houndstooth check and not a single drop. Scorched yellow
on forever. The step to counter desolation. The step to say,
"What's your rush?" New vertigo feelings. No lenses,
no glue, nothing. Then it's emptier. I'd be behind the letter.

Later I learned she could play piano by ear.

    That's her enterprise, I might say,

her dream of resistance. I shouldn't doubt so readily.

Calculating now what's permissible, and what
                                        we're barred from even considering.

So I stand from another vantage point, our train slips from view.

Lies themselves began to take me at my word

It's official: between her skull and the matchhead.
Only ordinary blackmail. And on the outskirts of town
it shapes up. Not available until trouble is. Everyone else
talks lying down. With the question I shouldered it. Otherwise
kept us tied. The zipper then the apple. On one condition.
Scared me through the windshield. The secretary deems it so.
It's our attention to the waves, the glare. Ends well in a close
summer. Again and again it was just enough. Louder than
spadework before lunch. A dry summer shimmer. We struck
more matches. Cooling on the avenue. She noted and tallied
what was fully alive, what mourned, what retired. Combed it out.
Plum flowers on dry paper. Plenty to know about soldiers.
Hiding in our skins while the sky is still on. Maybe it's made
of tin. Out in the summer, easier to imagine if they're propped
like fence posts. Heard and then if summer ends, another judge
and the flutter of banknotes. Even if I could grow sleeves
when it cools. Late, late and she by herself squeezed through.

I heard the dry objects of the mad people rustling

The wayside is there to teach. And if you so
much as glanced. Got stuck after the second line.
Entire lives made you—ah, thistles with a further
purpose. At the end, sinking. Then with the bullet,
the belt, he'd peel out. Be tip-top until we count
paces. And the cramming in of early autumn,
the sure cramming in. Roll toward the light queens. Say yes,
to trembling fruit. Oh, that's tip-top! When does
my skin fly open? And do clicks wish to grow back?
To be birch. Between banks. Apologize before swabbing
the deadwood. Out with the loose jacket, the tailor
declared. (My grandmother too, an excellent seamstress.)
For the landowners the thistles made a border right.
Then what's stuck? Linger when leaves slough off hands.
Everyone somewhere in the country. Tight squares.
You could wait to play. The tracks came to the end.
Queens stitched on. I'm reaching it, carrying provinces.
To be tree and promise not to. To be ice and win the hand.

I had called her up before the operation shut down.

                    Then I'd come clean,
her message pushed at a zigzag pace.

                              Some shaking to their finish.

She told me what to keep, what to break off.

The Vague Territory of the Present

Someone should make it
their business—
so we could transfer the meeting
pack it up, pinch it
into a needle's eye
to be seen through
a magnifying glass
and I'd take
the tin and pour vinegar
around the entrance
so no one
would think to forego
another supper
that's the feeling when
my lungs slip down
to my ankles
I knew it was misery,
like the dog said the misery
of broken chairs

and when we came
to the meridian
I slid the ruler
out of my dress
I had to tell her
to buckle myself
to the sky, then let her
provide the ledger
proof the day is alive—
in my head, I felt
the blows to her windpipe
I could no longer
hinder the outcome
I could only adjust my limbs
accordingly
but first I had to tongue
the glass gears
and count the empty drawers
to warrant a reprieve.

This morning they were flying low

Dishevelment in the chair. They sell at the best
places so cut her expression. Merely adrift or else beyond
the chair. So much like the table, her resolve. Inside,
yet neither makes it closer. Becoming chair, I could look
in circles. Like vinyl in the brain. No sky beyond
facial expressions. Neither was herself. The street
was real. Even so, don't you count the grass straws? Find
the one-eyed number where I'm caught scraping nearby.
Promise then, and crazy with the broom, yawn over offices.
He becomes the liability. Then rumors—short and tall—stick,
while nausea makes me soft. I envy her letter that snitches on
the chairs. Let go the little creatures. Officiate the forms
past hell. Neither could skip the outer shell. Headlong into daylight,
her backrest up so she could tell a bad lie. And the summons,
like chirping, like a new porcelain forehead. In centimeters
it grew closer to what it should. Wiping up the peeled pieces
with this money, I could hold off, I could lean them in that direction.

Then there's the complicit part

of the brain.

And I'm compelled

to theorize the problem

I glide into the range off-grid   duping them   parading a faux genre—

objects and plants, yes, but not a centerpiece,

even with all the passengers around.

Whose secrecy lapsed

No world outside. The radio blaring through the door.
So sulk with summer. Not that I'd forget. To check on
the morning nerves. Her signal from the window.
Like a mood that needs to unwind. To empty. Preferring
synthetics to security. Burned through to the other room.
I'd transfigure myself into a table or chest. The more
possible it became. Might seem commonplace. To bank all
we made. To walk outside while it's still habitable.
Didn't have it *in* me in the end. Not native like the purple
clover. She retained her plastic silhouette. Good to know
the race had started. More static, grew louder through
the transom. Soon the city turned around on her, insulting
without saying out loud. If it weren't for thunder or
the miracle. She'd offer her ears. She wiped the thicket clean.
Kept trying to lay her coat down. I wouldn't stay. Without cloth
for protection. Pushing forward, the door gleamed like scissors.

Distract yourself by counting entryways

Locked in an index file. Devised tokens for saving.
Blame it on not knowing her whereabouts. Your cue:
ask the dumb me. Set a foot there, blame that too.
Neither message came. Sometimes it's blindness.
Sometimes that's how the skin tightens. Not a hand wave,
just a lousy bet. Her legs pulled into her chest.
"Bottle green" they called the car. In between shadows
like lazy bats. Our train rolled on worries. Her sweater
opened like a door. That kind of green doesn't really
exist. I nearly drove it around. Out of hearing range, but where
does it lodge? Then so close you could see the pilot's face.
Currency, that's what keeps us steering. From then on
you'd jettison their response, hold on to your skin. Questions
of varying lengths. Could it be the third and fourth degree?
Possibly she's styled for travel. Possibly a blanket calling out.
Afterwards, a stiff push. I thought I'd speak or speed off.

I focused on a horizon above a dark disk.

Then the rhythm grew softer.
Things turned inside. I said it all then,
without quoting her and

shouldered the responsibility.

Defense was a runaway tactic

Hers is out of hand and rubbed to shreds. Crumbled into
translucent flakes. Any two-fold promise could seal it. A broad
injury, the plaintiff left behind. Try to maintain without access
to the mezzanine. Her neck pushed up again. In her own
words, the shock came with mid-winter sand. Heard about
it through telephone wars. Soft tyranny and trolling by
gadgets. Didn't have the open space. Start at low tide and
comb for shells and glass. Steel ringing in her collarbone.
Like a private balcony. A shred of the message blurred.
I never held her to it. Unless the orbit was mine. The lapsed
welcome seemed counterintuitive. She always talked
from the ground floor. Insisting on a view. Sources were what
she called for. Burden to what she never saw, and what could
the shore be anymore? The view gave way, the roads grew difficult
with guards. She's smoother than others. Smoother than glass.

After Something Else

I can open the side of her face
then, inspect the way
she chooses the motor to whir
then steer her
I cut the cloth
between our rooms
and fasten little circles
on the back of my neck
some oil leaks
out on the road
coating it where nettles
had been, she crosses
without her salty mask
bring a business model
they'd said and
present it on the table
then we had no choice
but to watch—

the suffering was quick
and her dress filled with
their remarks, popping threads,
a full blitz of things—
rolling and skidding
across the beams
no anesthetic
for either of us
but her words pulse
when they shove them
she can off this boredom
rev it and make it go
then, like a vision—
the magistrate wanders
through the foyer,
his prick has seen its days
I follow along pulling a rope
through hidden compartments
she buries a bulb
deep in the floor.

Only a fraction could be undone.

Who sent her?

Knowing the cases of blackmail. That she could then
cross over my threshold. That it was recorded,
maybe in the courtyard,

perhaps on the steps.

Left at the ceremony

Each letter was almost athletic—bold and winning.
I held them out from my face. No occupation
rivals it. So broad—the knack some have. Exiled.
Maybe we friended a century ago. Keen markings
you have there. Careful don't nudge for an answer.
Last census says, from ice-seller to landowner.
I barely saw the future behind us. Pull my own mouth
close to the floor. Could have poisoned the orchard.
She distilled some water on the wound. And soon
we came to the Agency for Eventuality then to the
Ombudsman for Futility. Held me in a ring of noise.
The top's bubbling. Towel off, and accept the law word.
Agree to the muffling and the flags on alert. Wasn't
angling for new. I had what was later built. A friend
swapped for a body. A category for matching fixtures.
Climb onto the furniture. Find something to treat it.

Give in to high costs

Nevertheless, it's valuable. Imagine she sunk it. Consider
the witnesses and all that you withstood. Flatter only
then. And the test about to be given. If a word
held court. It might loosen a seam. Like grand theft.
When to keep using. To augment guests. Right away,
a hierarchy begins. Try not to notice, look as if you know
the shareholders. Go blind if you fixed the price. Nothing like
yourself. Clamoring for it. Do they testify? Do they
sharpen their lips—get ready? Moving usurps listening.
Takes longer than considering, takes longer than choosing
a shade. Rescue if you fall into it. Use a cheat method.
More emerge out of the stairwell. Look at the scaffolding,
pretend it's the last ship out. Tranquil answers. Careful, they
sink fast. Shareholders begin to walk vertically. Reminded me of
my great aunt. Her blindness. And the steep stairs. The version
she might tell. Out of fear, divvy up the hooks then build.

She Shrank from Any Name

Protection's nearly
impossible when the train
lurches forward
my certain neighbor runs
toward the harbor today, *today*,
decked out
in metallic ribbons
she comes close
to the picket line,
she scrutinizes
the old-world politic—
hear the gavel
and gasps? would you park
under the linden trees?
even as the trial goes on
in my sitting room
I choose the traitor
don't count on the trees,
look away, as they look away

her shoulders weighted
and pinned
to the exam room
I stay awake and
in dim light I try
to view proceedings
without a weapon, without
something to make my hair
stiff, you could
hear her name
bouncing off every leaf
and the bluff wound
its way up from her knees
should I lurk
in this necropolis,
stay my clam self,
perched and closed
while she chills
with the night?
we were all so vigilant.

She suffered the corners everywhere,
          and readier than done.   A scrape on her cornea,

                                        and the sky broke into pieces.
What spins for
a fluttering second?   What birds she kept hearing?

Afterwards she swore
they caught the ferry.
                                             The bags, even folded,   kept buzzing inside.

Who was waving in the background?

When the roughness was over, so was the sentence

In high heels because they'd introduce me,
then knock into things. If they were dead already.
I'd clip the thumb and drink the rest. But can a beast
have a tooth and give it up? Give us a kiss when you grip
too hard. It's corn silk that shuts my eyes. Dwarfed
next to that one. Maybe you've gutted it, worked
the spare change out. From running outside the world
for so long. Pull your legs underneath. Take the nest,
the swear word, and what might hurt the news. When I'd
come back, spoons would glisten. Everything would
return bite-sized. Long been lucky and the much too thick.
Without embarrassment. Your heels didn't help with
a reply, the hat neither. No longer knew the house. Ceilings turn
with autumn for the umpteenth time. In death, still using, still
bearing the weight of it. Breathing like beetles in an attic.
Swallowing hard, I'd reconsider where all the defensives hid.

In the era of efforts

The millionth one under suspicion. Pressed it with
my heel anyway. Her pins in a row—no legs, no flight.
Held them tight between her lips. We had ferried over,
so goes the version. I had lessons coming, for weeks.
Made my rounds in the house. Dye left in a bowl and
the smearing that held fast. My palms revealed the hunted.
Everyone mentioned the smearing. A thread down her calf
and my feet anchored to the floor. Let's not be so fast
to forego the comfort. Like gasoline leaking from a cuff. So
the numb side of my face showed nicely. After all, the puffs
had disappeared. The iron arm of the up and down. Most pins
had their spaces. When it flattens out they sting more. Deliveries
came with the breakwater. Wasn't I elbowed when she left?
Jarring to think so. Engineered for tasks like that. What's Saturday
without it. An outcome of the dirty trip up North. So much
wedged in that tote. Her hair loose at the shoulder, sometimes idling.

That's the Moon Trying to Leave the City

and getting caught
on the border of night
politely I have to do it,
re-construct what I
didn't want
to know, the cipher delivers
the living—the few and
their sentences flip and
swell up. I had no
treatment for it,
we couldn't shield her
anymore, I know we're
at cross purposes
as the heads of orchids
keep time, turn cheeks
an opening was sprung
by a latch near her dresser,
and a breeze falters inside
my sternum, letting
the slow dispatch begin

our trade consisted
of a filthy tote bag for
a hairbrush
with this waking,
she values how easily
a new message can blow across
like ash, its vibrato
rising off the cement
now what costs
to be negotiated?
our building swelled
until our meeting
slid out, wait for
the sugary taste,
as threads hang from
her hem, and not
a lick of rain
on the steps, but the last hum
makes a stitch that
tingles in her sinuses,
darts around her head.

Wait to be called on

Weren't we going after the stranger? Shunt the mode.
Like a vintage radar installed. The noise my teeth made.
After they landed. Some with limbs, flesh. Electrodes near
a spine. Hazards solved in my head. What held me,
what I said. I'm compelled to straddle it. It had those
pieces of flesh. Hair in the mouth then a bee in the mouth.
Anything stuck in the head. And grief—over, fini, kaput.
If translated, it makes noise. I'm supposed to covet more.
So I framed it, then I framed it. The air shakes and
wind slaps. If we went along too fast, the shiver would
push it out. The backing-up fiasco arrives. Forgive me,
I edged too close. Be punctual. Light the flesh if the body
can be moved in a heap. Like one could crash into it.
Step through the list of side effects. My pretext left
sheepishly again. Here's the future: a sea of bargains.
And self—the song we push and button, and button again.

Her version trafficked   for so little.

An interrogative I might call sublime.

When you looked, you couldn't
see in   everything's reflected back.

Also, that she was locked
always, here, in an interminable present.

Preponderance of evidence

When aid came it was tomorrow. Pulling snaps apart,
I'd rather wing it. Had that one claim. Ticked and tocked
it around her head. Strategies compounded the underside.
Warned as she tried to deny. There was hearsay, we compromised.
We'd predict her next blank space. Speak to me as if I have
Zorro's mask on. Then I'm a late baby boomer, but not
dependent that way. Even the zinnia bed was kept under
wraps. Thick with gnats, thick with new lettering. I'd invent
a stitch for my sentence so its pulse would skip. When she
finally revealed her jagged hairline. Shh-sounds came
intermittently with the rainfall. Facts inside the matchbook
spoke to it. In exchange for a clean-up crew. I brought wings
to cover my face. Supposing they'd excavate soon. Warships
in the afternoon, warships in the evening. Strike and stay
if they don't believe. A session goes unheeded. Over the speaker
a muddied voice re-tells the score. Slip like it got waxed
and knew anyway. Drive like your rescue came too soon.

Visualize Anyone

She understood it now,
the cog behind her back,
celebrated it, even,
as her arms hung
down too far
her makeup too was amplified
feel the grooves
and teeth, if the cube
she lived in would break,
the shiny walls
would stoop and
bow—that's why
I pulled her words in tight,
even words that blistered
without a remedy
I anticipated her testimony,
that sustained me

when the crows
increased, it was time for
the sky to stretch
the group would never
surrender so I brought
the starving ones
milk, it helped them
burn a path
it's not English
anymore, and when
her scarves rose
higher than the elms,
they snapped like shellfish
and filled it all with noise
she held her blouse up
to my ear—listen, if you don't
wear gray, the sunlight will
bury you, I read
her next epic in a day.

Eternal argument, my ancestry

Somewhere it was leaking. We had our theories—took
the lead from a wolf. Held it under my nose. That's how
climbing the rafters proved helpful. What could evidence say
if it was a pact or a spy thing. They made a poor showing
of it. Because I'm attached. Located near the crawl space.
Unsettling, systems broke down. Planets bulging when you
look closer at the synapses. An afterimage powders the
sheen away. Questioned hundreds of times. Would he even
be a suspect if they were absorbed into the proscenium?
Legend has it that the sea gives up its debris. Scatters without
a plan. And looking at my matrilineage, I'd fall into that group.
Assume more sounds were audible. A grimace signals
foreign voices. What particular gravity does she trust? Press
down to listen. I'm the richer for it. Like a mess full of wind.
The attic beams hesitate. Give in. As wind blows and pleads
behind our ears. Emptying more proves it. Small gears left inside.

The Busiest Body

I'm lucky, ghostly lucky,
when I start roaming
and recognize the sign
on the building's door
fenced in now,
what a dirty morning—
scabs on the chairs,
weeds, with their machine
hearts, whining
and the air would shrink,
draw up into my stomach
and settle in a nest
of glass, I'd later
find my sweat
all over town, she'd
counseled me before:
wait for the gears
to click, wait for
the buzz through the ground

without a flinch,
she took the bet, and I had
a giddy sense that
what remained
would be delivered
the tip of her ear dripped,
staining her collar,
the elm drips, the earth drips
she pinched a talon
and held it out to me
wise up, I'd tried to say,
and my ears filled like pockets
how do I register myself?
am I beating?
is air leaving my mouth?
there's minutiae—
glue drying in corners,
arms held down with string.

She'd almost admit his whereabouts

from thirty years ago.
Meaning to ask— needed to ask it,

until they looked at
themselves.

Her entire face dissolved,

as if there was no function in it,
though undercurrents were visible,
as if the answer squirmed close to the surface.

Easy solution for alteration

Easier to focus on the screen door than the tailpipe.
Instead, I'm lying in wait. Or I pull up the ladder. When
letting someone else slip off. I've entered the stranger's
torso. Retreat is nothing if not harnessed. A new brand
glows. If she had her hand out, flecks would drift down.
Can history lock in my throat this way? Not starving stacks up
to not lying. Might consider a tighter method. Instructions
embedded in my elbows. In order to move in circles. In order
for a waiting period to stay idle. Double down when she led
and heaped on the flattery. Later withered under the look.
Clogged with rules. Fit them snugly around the head. Follow
to pluck splinters. Record the upstarts, treasonous or not.
Heal nicely then. She'd cover for me. She with a penchant
for glove wearing. Take them from any stranger. After pelvis
and spine. We built moods. Found them swimming alone.

I myself. I couldn't get past those two words for a long time. I myself. Who was that. Which of the multiple beings from which "myself" was composed?

Christa Wolf

Barbara's Turn

(after the German film Barbara, *dir. Christian Petzold)*

Without signs. And her body is summoned. Her skirt's equilibrium glides and steadies her.

Andre (the chief physician) and the Stasi officer stand at the window, looking down at her as she arrives. The white curtains brush the white radiator.

Even at this distance. Her slight unease. Her detachment draws a slim, invisible line to elsewhere. Do I adjust my thinking as I move closer?

"You already know where I live," she says to Andre, "You've been groomed." She smirks and faces him with her hardest eyes.

And I sense the predicament, and I wince at another kind of punishment. But it's nothing to do with me. In this network that tightens and turns.

"Here's where I separate," she says. Down her dirt path. The leaning sunflowers, rustling leaves, again in lingering green.

She's certain, methodical. And no. There's no rousing music, no notes to punctuate or dissipate the tension.

And quiet disables. So many qualifying quiets. Quiet beneath the surface. It's as if windows themselves stare out, gaping, from the peeling paint.

If I could stand dead center, there'd be nothing. Only the dirt path. Leaves turning, shifting with each gust.

Tedium like another day. She fetches her bike from the cellar. Rides again to a secret. A secret place to collect money. Voices recede. The breeze stirs and stirs.

Humming precedes the car motor. Bike rattling precedes shoes on the walkway.

Questions stack gradually. The hospital is her place of solace, respect. Discretion. Her value is certain here. This juvenile ward is a place of banishment for her.

Can I predict what she'll do? Can I see the other side as she does? What does she explain to herself in a hypothetical life?

Dry indecision. And it seems bankrupt now through the halls and swinging doors of her hospital. Though the young woman patient belongs to Barbara.

Stella she's called, and Barbara repeats her name. Her hopelessness Barbara comprehends, as Stella has escaped again from a labor camp. What to consider? Do I pause here?

Barbara's confidence in her own skill spreads out into the halls, windows, spans a life, spans a space between stones and train stop, between what is grounded and what is adrift.

I sense the sea air in this small town by the Baltic. I don't see the sea, but feel its hum. Barbara surfaces in order to help Stella and, by her bed, reads to her from a novel,

"They follow the track of that sackful of rocks to the shore."

Gravity comes like a defense now. Her longing is sucked up in the fading light of the dirt path. She's expert. But they systematically follow.
They know her movements.

There's a brief tryst with her lover from the West. Distance seems in her favor for the better part of an hour. I see he's stylish, well-dressed. The two seem to lie in softness together.

I want to believe that she will be with this man, that it's her desire, even as he mentions she won't have to work when she's together with him. A stiff silence here as she considers.

Then the camera and the view shift. I'm startled in the darkness, as she rides her bike back. "Had a little outing?" His car swerves around her, brakes hard.

Another man searches her apartment, her blouses on hangers, as she smokes. A woman snaps on rubber gloves. "This way." The banality, and a whisper plea from Barbara. "Bend over, spread your legs," the woman says.

A view of her table with ashtray, red cosmetic case, sugar bowl. Still the current from the sea is not detectable. The expensive cigarettes from her lover.

And such lateness. Seething beneath. And on the train others stare. In the hallway, others linger. A mere trace of watching, following.

I sense the sea air. And I know she sees her way out. I have an image of her lover who desires her. How does the pacing put me there? Inside her determination.

Rustling leaves. White curtain and tyranny of her stovepipe and sink. A rhyme of curtain, her white medical jacket. The shrubs along the path.

Barbara knows the brutality that would come to Stella, who she discovers is pregnant. Knowing what would befall her.

What does Andre reveal of himself? Does she see his betrayal? His lot, as she calls it. Or now, does Andre? I've learned of her compassion. The things to fill in—to fill in place of freedom?

Her belatedness. His interest in her. Lateness and particles rise from the dirt road as she bicycles past. The late falls into more lateness. The branches rustle again in the changing day, then dusk.

What can I read in Barbara's posture? Her long neck. Loose hair falling from her bun. "I was not to be found," she says.

A vantage point I have. I know her escape is imminent.

It's more than halfway through the film, and I hear from the radio in the hospital *Serenade for Strings* by Tchaikovsky. Is this the first time there is music?

And it's the ballet music I love. And I think now this film *is* a ballet. The rows of dancers, crescents of skirts—their afterimage. Roiling then exhaling.

And what stirs beneath the coolness—a threat, a pitch of longing then consent? Something *must.* It's that systematic. The rushing and urgency. And Stella.

A duplicate of Barbara. Yet the girl is nothing like Barbara. No one is, and so she has to make another. And hides more money.

Who would be humiliated later? Now, with the sea, there's summoning. Black waves and moonlit foam. Noise of rushing water overlays their voices.

Her chance at freedom.

The girl must go. Barbara puts a purse around this girl's neck. Barbara's hair, lit strands and the sea foam. Mirroring. Some is what she knows.

And here I struggle. Is it a sacrifice? Is it an impulsive choice? Is it weariness?

The skin diver and Barbara quickly help Stella onto a raft. Rushing and tipping waves. Some of it must be more than freedom. Barbara bargains, she trades.

The rims of white sea foam, like the edges of an eclipse or a skirt. A half-life is hers. Strands of lighter gray and silver. Whose turn is it now? No narrative is clear, no purpose looms with certainty. One replaces another. One shifts in the breeze. An escape that won't be hers again.

The space between each wave and strand of white. The sea halts and contracts as Barbara returns to shore, steps from the water toward the dark sea grass.

In the Intrepid Life

When signals lapse
she sleuths the numbers out—
the daily lie
even then, we're swallowing
the routine after
it was broken, her eyes
turn to aluminum
under the fumes
I could only speak
through my veil of skin—
milky and spoiling
just need to
withstand the racket
and master
the code switch
my brain
now all scrubbed
easily slides on the tray

prepare a eulogy,
a marriage of splinters
and coins, she'd say
that it's customary
I see the symmetry
in her tastes as
I head for the upper floor
(there's a hook there
to hang my ribs on)
all afternoon
I confused her pallor
with concentration
nothing could bid us away,
her eyes roving over the data
withering then,
I give the nerve speech,
that is to say, I press
the right letters.

Hide well along with weapons

I guarded myself with a thimble. Hums seep through
the entryway. And waves keep a semblance of
something public. We were all so busy, so very busy.
Since valves got closed. Some failed outright. And she
carried the last sweater with dictation. Marked as proof
of habit. This launch being so fast. It's good to signal longingly
to your forebears. Obliged to do the holiday thing. Wasn't
that with lightning speed. Denied access to the mail. To track
down and cauterize it after. Our map lied to us, like a nerve
in a sack. Hear her out. Not to cast judgment on her exiting
forearms. As her table featured wooden dice. She stretched
the frame. Sought out earphones. If it had been vulgar, how
does she show up? Slightly. As a hooligan. With threads
crisscrossed at the sternum. We're faced with theater. With
skin intact and without a railing. Animal enough to hold it all in.

Know the measurement comes with a cost

As if an adjective could lose out. I won't mistake
excursion for devotion. Likely called a quarrel. When
my DIY garden surges success. Air whooshes by. Most
leaves blow in fan shapes. Starting in one zone and ending
with mosses labeled. Covet the crannies between. Whether
a die-off had begun. I'm in full-body wool. Who's been a fake
in the days before. Boundaries came loose. Not because I was
trained. But because others established swagger. Reaching
the point of sensors shutting down. She needs a ticket again.
To auction items that seemed ghostly. Nothing remedies
that. She could turn tree. She could source the flocking.
If what began as hiding became filled with magnetism. Why
tangle with outliers? Take the whole chorus along with muscles.
Tighter on her index finger. The questions lacked gratitude.
When I keep hearing beeps. Not even reckless. She'd be
assembled. With highlights on the borders. A field arraigned.

Someone else's liabilities

I'm nearly sucked into the early season. Along with fresh
linen. No hurry if we knew where. Where to twist the wires.
We're not made for surrender. With circling wrens just as
popular. Other fauna close to our noses. Found moving
in slow motion worked. Could make it out scot-free. If we
tore past the night yard. Then be robbed of it. Better to
skim than to fret. Slated for planting. Some brought a beeline
to the memorial. Like the train schedule said. No languishing
in their shade. Our yard in sync with the source. Not nearly
forgiven. With less traffic to decipher. Heard buzzing before
the pageant. And the tenure of house sparrows. Maybe if
we licked it clean. Until a numb layer appeared between us
and the rest. Learning to register the electric current. She'd
memorize why we came. It slips through the leaning branch.
Discover what's buried. Somehow never making it across.

Late Meeting under the Bridge

As I rummage through my neck, I hit the pauses—
                a shady spot, a nerve knot.

Then she instructs how to. Don't hurry,
the dust will cloud

into an oblong shape,
    a kidney. And I can pilfer
some pathetic

                magpie treasures,
use my elbows
as weapons. And how is it,

we're still afraid
                of streets changing names,
of broken power lines

    shocked and shivering?
She memorized our path,

yet no real route is clear, no

hives to live in.
Industrial fortitude—
                she had it, as she had

her tight-waist look
today. I want a train
of expressions,

their best deceptions,
tassels with fake laughs.
I expected the window to fall,

the force of air to rush,
pull us down.
Our collars snug as we re-enter,

then it's the fall
with fear, and in my neck I tighten the fear.

Where's the thinking?
I asked where,

until panic sucked us down to the ground.
Rummaging couldn't be done,

couldn't be as we thought.
Where were our nerves?

Wasn't it when we hurried?
If dust clouded up,
I couldn't see any weapons,

except a mirror stuck in my arm,
couldn't even visualize them.

We had some qualms, we twitched lightly,
specters of smallness looking back.
                And if we took the instructions—

were they hers, what name, whose
do I laugh at?
            The tasks—
the tasks regard us and we could be shivering

and fall under, be hidden with shards

underneath, not to be seen.
We could
                surrender, we could give chase.

ACKNOWLEDGMENTS

Thank you to the editors of the following journals in which these poems first appeared, sometimes in different versions:

Bennington Review, Boston Review, The Canary, Datableed, Interim, Lana Turner, Laurel Review, New American Writing, Recliner Magazine, Volt.

Inspirations and notes:
—the German film *Barbara* directed by Christian Petzold
—*The Appointment* by Herta Müller (trans. by Michael Hulse and Philip Boehm)
—*The Fox Was Ever the Hunter* by Herta Müller (trans. by Philip Boehm)
—*The Quest for Christa T.* by Christa Wolf (trans. by Christopher Middleton)
—*What Remains and Other Stories* by Christa Wolf (trans. by Heike Schwarzbauer and Rick Takvorian)

With gratitude to many friends for their support and generosity over the years—Susan Segal, Gail Wronsky, Michelle Latiolais, Karen Kevorkian, Judith Taylor, Rodney Jones, Francesca Lia Block, Calvin Bedient, Martha Ronk, Claire Dougherty, and John O'Brien.

And thank you to Vivienne for your inspiration and love.
And to Daniel, my endless gratitude for all of your love, your insights, and your adventures.
And many thanks to Laura, Rusty, Sophia and all the staff at Omnidawn.

Molly Bendall was born in Richmond, Virginia. She is the author of five previous collections of poetry, including *Watchful* from Omnidawn and *Under the Quick* from Parlor Press. Her chapbook of translations of the Egyptian-French poet Joyce Mansour appeared from Toad Press (2022). She has won the Eunice Tietjens Prize from *Poetry*, The Lynda Hull Award from *Denver Quarterly*, and two Pushcart Prizes. She teaches English and Creative Writing at the University of Southern California.

Turncoat
by Molly Bendall

Cover art by John O'Brian
Cover design by Laura Joakimson
Cover typeface: Abril Fatface and Academy Engraved LET

Interior design by Laura Joakimson and Sophia Carr
Interior typeface: Garamond Premier Pro

Printed in the United States
by Books International, Dulles, Virginia
Acid Free Archival Quality Recycled Paper

Publication of this book was made possible in part by gifts from
Katherine & John Gravendyk in honor of Hillary Gravendyk,
Francesca Bell, Mary Mackey, and New Place Fund